PRESENTS

THE ULTIMATE BOOK OF

SUPER FUNNY

GAME-WINNING

SPORTS
JOKES

FOR KIDS

AND WORLD CHAMPIONS!

BY WORDPLAY GROUNDHOG

CONTENTS

BASKETBALL
JOKES

WHY CAN'T BASKETBALL PLAYERS GO ON VACATION?

BECAUSE THEY AREN'T ALLOWED TO TRAVEL!

WHY DID THE COACH WANT A JUDGE ON HIS BASKETBALL TEAM?

TO BRING ORDER TO THE COURT!

WHAT DOES A BASKETBALL GENIE GIVE YOU?

THREE SWISHES!

WHAT DO YOU CALL A BASKETBALL NET IN HAWAII?

A HULA HOOP!

WHERE WILL YOU FIND ARTISTS ON A BASKETBALL COURT?

IN THE PAINT!

WHAT IS THE DIFFERENCE BETWEEN BALL HOGS AND TIME?

TIME PASSES!

**WHAT CAN YOU GET
IN A BASKETBALL STORE
WITHOUT ANY MONEY?**

A FREE THROW!

**WHY DIDN'T THE SKELETON MAKE
THE BASKETBALL TEAM?**

IT DIDN'T HAVE ANY HEART!

**WHAT DO YOU CALL A BOAT FULL OF
POLITE BASKETBALL PLAYERS?**

A GOOD SPORTSMAN-SHIP!

WHAT IS IT CALLED WHEN A BASKETBALL PLAYER MISSES A DUNK?

ALLEY OOPS!

BASEBALL JOKES

HOW CAN YOU PITCH A WINNING BASEBALL GAME WITHOUT THROWING A BALL?

ONLY THROW STRIKES!

WHAT IS THE BEST ADVICE YOU CAN GIVE A BASEBALL PLAYER?

IF YOU DON'T SUCCEED AT FIRST, TRY SECOND BASE!

WHY DOES A PITCHER RAISE ONE LEG WHEN HE THROWS THE BALL?

IF HE RAISES BOTH LEGS, HE WILL FALL DOWN!

WHY DID THE POLICE OFFICER GO TO THE BASEBALL GAME?

SOMEONE WAS STEALING BASES!

WHAT IS THE BEST POSITION IN BASEBALL FOR A CRAB?

PINCH HITTER!

WHY IS IT HARD TO STEAL THIRD BASE?

BECAUSE OF THE SHORT STOP ON THE WAY!

WHY DON'T BASEBALL PLAYERS LOCK THEIR DOORS?

THEY ARE ALWAYS SAFE AT HOME!

WHY DO DOGS LOVE PLAYING BASEBALL?

THEY ALWAYS GET WALKED!

WHY DID THE BASEBALL COACH WANT A SINGER ON HIS TEAM?

BECAUSE OF THE SINGER'S PERFECT PITCH!

WHY DO CATCHERS HAVE THE SHORTEST DRIVE TO WORK?

THEY WORK AT HOME!

FOOTBALL JOKES

WHERE DO HUNGRY FOOTBALL PLAYERS WANT TO PLAY?

IN THE SUPPER BOWL!

WHAT DO YOU CALL THE SON OF AN OFFENSIVE LINEMAN?

A CHIP OFF THE OLD BLOCKER!

WHY WAS THE FOOTBALL COACH YELLING AT A VENDING MACHINE?

IT WOULDN'T GIVE HIM HIS QUARTER-BACK!

WHO HAS THE SMELLIEST POSITION IN FOOTBALL?

THE SCENTER!

WHICH FOOTBALL PLAYER HAS STRONG LEGS AND BUILDS HOUSES?

THE CAR-PUNTER!

HOW ARE FOOTBALL PLAYERS ALWAYS READY FOR HALLOWEEN?

THEY ALREADY HAVE FACE MASKS!

WHY DON'T FOOTBALL PLAYERS WEAR GLASSES?

IT'S A CONTACT SPORT!

WHY DID THE FOOTBALL COACH PUT A NINJA IN THE GAME?

TO RUN A SNEAK PLAY!

WHY DID THE QUARTERBACK WALK OFF THE FIELD?

THE COACH TOLD HIM TO TAKE A HIKE!

WHY DO FOOTBALL COACHES LIKE KICKERS?

THEY PUT THEIR BEST FOOT FORWARD!

SOCCER JOKES

WHY DO SOCCER PLAYERS DO SO WELL IN SCHOOL?

THEY KNOW HOW TO USE THEIR HEADS!

HOW DID THE SOCCER GOALIE GET RICH?

SHE LOVED TO SAVE!

WHY WAS THE SOCCER PLAYER UPSET ON HIS BIRTHDAY?

HE GOT A RED CARD!

WHY COULD NOBODY
SEE THE SOCCER BALL?

THE DEFENSE CLEARED IT!

27

**WHY DID THE COACH
PUT A MAGICIAN IN
THE SOCCER GAME?**

**HE WAS THE BEST
AT HAT TRICKS!**

**HOW DO YOU KNOW
SOCCER REFEREES
LOVE THEIR JOB?**

**THEY WHISTLE
WHILE THEY WORK!**

WHY WAS THE SOCCER FIELD SHAPED LIKE A TRIANGLE?

SOMEBODY TOOK A CORNER!

WHY WAS THE PIG EJECTED FROM THE SOCCER GAME?

FOR PLAYING DIRTY!

WHY WAS THE SOCCER STADIUM SO WINDY?

IT WAS FULL OF FANS!

WHY DO ARTISTS CHEER FOR THE SOCCER TEAM THAT IS LOSING?

THEY WANT THE GAME TO END IN A DRAW!

HOCKEY
JOKES

WHY DO HOCKEY RINKS HAVE CURVED CORNERS?

IF THEY WERE 90 DEGREES, THE ICE WOULD MELT!

WHAT HAPPENED TO THE HOCKEY PLAYER WHO WANTED A PAY RAISE?

THEY GAVE HIM A CHECK!

WHY DIDN'T THE HOCKEY PLAYER HAVE A GOOD GAME?

HE GOT COLD FEET!

**WHAT DO HOCKEY PLAYERS
DRINK ON HOT DAYS?**

ICED TEA!

**WHAT DID THE COACH SAY
TO THE NEW HOCKEY PLAYER?**

I HAVE MY ICE ON YOU!

**WHY DON'T HOCKEY PLAYERS
LIKE BIRTHDAY CAKE?**

THEY THINK ICING IS BAD!

DO YOU KNOW WHAT AN ENFORCER DOES ON A HOCKEY TEAM?

JUST CHECKING!

WHEN DO HOCKEY PLAYERS WEAR ARMOR?

WHEN THEY PLAY KNIGHT GAMES!

WHAT JOB DID THE HOCKEY PLAYER GET AFTER HE STOPPED PLAYING?

AN OFF-ICE JOB!

WHAT DID THE HOCKEY GOALIE SAY TO THE PUCK?

CATCH YOU LATER!

GOLF JOKES

WHY DO GOLFERS ALWAYS CARRY AN EXTRA PAIR OF PANTS WITH THEM?

IN CASE THEY GET A HOLE IN ONE!

WHAT DOES A GOLFER'S DIET CONSIST OF?

A LOT OF GREENS AND SOME WATER!

WHERE CAN YOU FIND A GOLFER ON A SATURDAY NIGHT?

CLUBBING!

WHAT IS A GOLFER'S FAVORITE BIRD?

ANY BIRDIE ON A GOLF COURSE!

HOW MANY GOLFERS DOES IT TAKE TO CHANGE A LIGHT BULB?

FORE!

WHY COULDN'T THE GOLFER LISTEN TO MUSIC?

BECAUSE HE BROKE A RECORD!

WHAT IS A GOLFER'S WORST NIGHTMARE?

THE BOGEYMAN!

WHY DID THE GOLFER ALWAYS KEEP AN UMBRELLA NEARBY?

IN CASE OF A BAD "FORE" CAST!

WHAT SHOULD YOU DO IF YOU'RE BAD AT GOLF?

JOIN THE CLUB!

WHY ARE COMPUTERS SO GOOD AT GOLF?

THEY HAVE HARD DRIVES!

TENNIS JOKES

WHY WAS THE
TENNIS COURT SO LOUD?

**BECAUSE ALL THE PLAYERS
RAISED A RACKET!**

WHY DO TENNIS PLAYERS
HAVE LOW SELF-ESTEEM?

**BECAUSE THEY HAVE
SO MANY FAULTS!**

WHY SHOULD YOU NEVER FALL IN LOVE WITH A TENNIS PLAYER?

TO THEM, "LOVE" MEANS NOTHING!

**WHEN DOES A BRITISH
TENNIS MATCH END?**

WHEN IT'S WIMBLE-DONE!

**WHAT TIME DO
TENNIS PLAYERS GO TO BED?**

TENNISH!

**WHICH AMERICAN TENNIS
TOURNAMENT NEVER CLOSES?**

THE U.S. OPEN!

WHAT IS THE HARDEST TENNIS LESSON TO LEARN?

YOU CAN NEVER BE AS GOOD AS A WALL!

WHICH STATE HAS THE MOST TENNIS PLAYERS?

TENNIS-EE!

WHAT CAN YOU SERVE AT A TENNIS MATCH BUT NEVER EAT?

A TENNIS BALL!

WHY ARE FISH BAD TENNIS PLAYERS?

THEY DON'T LIKE GETTING CLOSE TO A NET!

SNOWBOARDING & SKIING JOKES

WHAT DO YOU CALL A SLOW SNOW SKIER?

A SLOPE-POKE!

WHAT DO SNOWBOARDERS LOVE TO EAT?

ICEBERGERS AND CHILLY DOGS!

HOW DO SKIERS GET TO SCHOOL?

BY ICICLE!

HOW DO SNOWBOARDERS PAY THEIR BILLS?

WITH COLD HARD CASH!

WHY SHOULDN'T YOU FIGHT ON A SKI LIFT?

IT'S AN UPHILL BATTLE!

WHY DID THE SNOWBOARDER EXPECT THE WORST WHEN HE REACHED THE TOP OF THE MOUNTAIN?

HE KNEW IT WAS ALL DOWNHILL FROM THERE!

WHAT DID THE HONEST SNOWBOARDER SAY WHEN HE WAS TOLD TO CHEAT?

SNOW WAY MAN!

WHERE DO SNOWBOARDERS KEEP THEIR MONEY?

IN A SNOW BANK!

WHERE DO YOUNG COWS SNOWBOARD?

ON A CALF-PIPE!

WHAT FALLS ON A SKI SLOPE BUT NEVER GETS HURT?

SNOW!

SWIMMING JOKES

WHAT KIND OF RACE IS NEVER RUN?

A SWIMMING RACE!

WHERE DO ZOMBIES GO SWIMMING?

THE DEAD SEA!

WHAT IS A SHEEP'S FAVORITE SWIM STROKE?

THE BAAAACKSTROKE!

WHAT IS THE BEST EXERCISE FOR A SWIMMER?

POOL-UPS!

WHAT DID THE OCEAN SAY TO THE SWIMMER?

NOTHING. IT JUST WAVED!

WHY DID THE VEGETARIANS STOP SWIMMING?

THEY DON'T LIKE MEETS!

WHAT WORD LOOKS THE SAME BACKWARDS AND UPSIDE DOWN?

SWIMS!

HOW DO SWIMMERS CLEAN THEMSELVES?

THEY WASH UP ON SHORE!

WHY WERE THE ELEPHANTS THROWN OUT OF THE SWIM MEET?

BECAUSE THEY COULDN'T KEEP THEIR TRUNKS UP!

WHY DID THE TEACHER JUMP INTO THE POOL?

SHE WANTED TO TEST THE WATER!

AUTO RACING JOKES

WHAT DO YOU CALL A CHEESEBURGER IN A RACE CAR?

FAST FOOD!

WHAT IS A DRIVER'S LEAST FAVORITE MEAL?

BRAKE-FAST!

WHY COULDN'T THE BICYCLE ENTER THE CAR RACE?

IT WAS TWO TIRED!

WHY DID EVERYONE LOOK AWAY WHEN THE RACE CAR DROVE PAST?

IT HAD A SPOILER ON IT!

WHAT DID THE TORNADO SAY TO THE RACE CAR?

WANT TO GO FOR A SPIN?

WHAT HAPPENS IF YOU RUN BEHIND A RACE CAR?

YOU GET EXHAUST-ED!

WHAT DO YOU GET WHEN YOU RUN IN FRONT OF A CAR?

TIRED!

WHY DO CLUB DJS MAKE TERRIBLE DRIVERS?

THEY KEEP CHANGING TRACKS!

WHY ARE RACECAR DRIVERS GREAT AT CHOOSING FRIENDS?

THEY'RE TRAINED TO LOOK FOR RED FLAGS!

WHAT DO YOU CALL IT WHEN DINOSAURS CRASH CARS?

TYRANNOSAURUS WRECKS!

RUNNING JOKES

WHY CAN'T YOU HEAR RUNNERS WHEN THEY'RE TRAINING?

THEY WEAR SNEAKERS!

WHAT SHOULD SLOW RUNNERS EAT BEFORE A BIG RACE?

FAST FOOD!

WHAT DO YOU CALL A LONG CAT RACE?

A MEOW-ATHON!

HOW DO YOU GET A RUNNER TO REMEMBER YOU?

JOG THEIR MEMORY!

HOW DO FIREFLIES START A RACE?

**ON YOUR MARK.
GET SET.
GLOW!**

WHY COULDN'T THE DOG RUN IN THE MARATHON?

BECAUSE HE WASN'T A PART OF THE HUMAN RACE!

WHAT DO SPRINTERS EAT BEFORE A RACE?

NOTHING. THEY FAST!

WHAT DID THE TOMATO TELL THE OTHER TOMATO DURING A RACE?

KETCHUP!

WHAT DO YOU CALL A SLOW RUNNER WITH A BAD BACK?

A SORE LOSER!

WHY WAS THE RUNNER STOPPED AND TAKEN TO JAIL?

HE WAS RESISTING A REST!

GYMNASTICS JOKES

WHICH SEASONS ARE BEST FOR GYMNASTICS?

HAND-SPRING AND SUMMER-SAULTS!

WHERE DO CHEATING GYMNASTS GO?

BEHIND PARALLEL BARS!

WHY DID THE GYMNAST STOP DRINKING COFFEE?

SHE WAS ALREADY TOO JUMPY!

HOW LONG DID IT TAKE FOR THE GYMNAST TO GET TO PRACTICE?

A SPLIT SECOND!

WHY DID THE GYMNAST BRING A TRAMPOLINE TO HER TEAM MEETING?

TO BOUNCE IDEAS OFF EVERYONE!

WHY DID THE GYMNAST BECOME A BODY BUILDER?

TO INCREASE THEIR FLEX-ABILITY!

DID YOU HEAR ABOUT THE ANGRY GYMNAST?

SHE JUST FLIPPED!

WHAT IS A BANANA'S FAVORITE GYMNASTICS MOVE?

THE SPLITS!

WHAT DID ONE GYMNAST SAY TO THE OTHER?

NICE TO MEET YOU!

DID YOU HEAR ABOUT THE GYMNAST WHO OPENED A BAKERY?

HER ROLLS ARE UNBEATABLE!

MARTIAL ARTS JOKES

WHY DID THE MARTIAL ARTS TEACHER GET INTO TROUBLE?

HE HAD A BAD SENSEI OF HUMOR!

WHAT IS A MARTIAL ARTIST'S FAVORITE PART OF A JOKE?

THE PUNCH LINE!

WHAT DO YOU CALL IT WHEN A MARTIAL ARTIST BREAKS A BOARD?

A SMASHING SUCCESS!

WHAT DO YOU CALL A LAWYER WHO KNOWS MARTIAL ARTS?

A SELF-DEFENSE ATTORNEY!

**WHAT DO YOU CALL A PIG
THAT DOES MARTIAL ARTS?**

PORKCHOP!

**WHAT DO YOU CALL A SHEEP
THAT DOES MARTIAL ARTS?**

LAMBCHOP!

**WHY DID THE MARTIAL ARTIST
BRING A LADDER TO THE FIGHT?**

**TO REACH NEW HEIGHTS
WITH HIS KICKS!**

VOLLEYBALL JOKES

WHY COULDN'T THE TWINS PLAY VOLLEYBALL?

THEY ALREADY HAD A MATCH!

WHY DID THE VOLLEYBALL PLAYER THINK HER SERVE WAS BROKEN?

THE OTHER TEAM ALWAYS RETURNED IT!

HOW DO VOLLEYBALL PLAYERS CELEBRATE?

WITH A BLOCK PARTY!

WHY DID THE VOLLEYBALL PLAYER LOSE HER JOB AT A RESTAURANT?

SOMEBODY ASKED HER TO SERVE THE FOOD!

WHAT RUNS ON THE EDGE OF A VOLLEYBALL COURT BUT NEVER MOVES?

THE SIDELINE!

WHY IS LOSING AT BEACH VOLLEYBALL WORSE ON HOT DAYS?

DE-FEET HURTS ON HOT SAND!

WHY ARE POLICE OFFICERS GREAT VOLLEYBALL PLAYERS?

THEY ARE TRAINED TO SERVE AND PROTECT!

BOWLING JOKES

WHY DID THE BOWLING BALL KEEP GETTING INTO TROUBLE?

IT HAD A BAD ROLL MODEL!

WHY DID THE BOWLER WAIT SO LONG TO TAKE THEIR TURN?

THEY WERE WAITING FOR INSPIRATION TO STRIKE!

WHY DID THE BOWLING COACH WANT A BASEBALL PLAYER ON THEIR TEAM?

BECAUSE HE THREW SO MANY STRIKES!

HOW DO YOU KNOW A BOWLING ALLEY IS QUIET?

YOU CAN HEAR A PIN DROP!

HOW MUCH SHOULD ONE GAME OF BOWLING COST?

TEN PINNIES!

WHAT IS THE WORST BOWLING JOKE?

NEVERMIND, I'LL SPARE YOU!

WHY DID THE BOWLER PLAY ANOTHER GAME?

HE HAD TIME TO SPARE!

**WHAT DID ONE
ROMANTIC BOWLING PIN
SAY TO THE OTHER?**

LET'S NEVER SPLIT!

**WHAT KIND OF BOWLING TEAM
CRIES WHEN IT LOSES?**

A BOWLING BAWL CLUB!

**WHAT DO BOWLING PINS DO WHEN
THEY ARE UNHAPPY AT WORK?**

THEY GO ON STRIKE!

ESPORTS JOKES

**WHY DO ESPORTS
GAMERS ALWAYS HAVE
A PLAN FOR THE FUTURE?**

THEY PLAY THE LONG GAME!

**WHAT DOES AN ESPORTS
GAMER USE TO MAKE BREAD?**

NINTEN-DOUGH!

**WHY DID THE ESPORTS
GAMER EAT HIS COMPUTER?**

HE WANTED TO HAVE A BYTE!

HOW DO YOU KNOW WHEN A PARTY IS FOR AN ESPORTS GAMER?

THERE ARE TONS OF STREAMERS!

**WHY DID THE ESPORTS GAMER
BREAK UP WITH HIS GIRLFRIEND?**

**THEY WEREN'T ON
THE SAME LEVEL!**

**WHY DID THE ESPORTS GAMER PLAY
VIDEO GAMES AFTER HIS BREAKUP?**

TO CONSOLE HIMSELF!

**WHY DID THE GAMER BRING
SHOES TO THE CONSOLE?**

**IN CASE IT NEEDED
TO REBOOT!**

WRESTLING JOKES

WHAT IS A WRESTLER'S FAVORITE VEGETABLE?

AN ARTI-CHOKE!

HOW DO WRESTLERS KEEP THEIR BIKES SECURE?

HEADLOCKS!

WHY COULDN'T THE LOSING WRESTLER LIGHT HIS GRILL?

HE LOST ALL OF HIS MATCHES!

WHICH SEASON MAKES WRESTLERS NERVOUS?

FALL!

WHAT'S THE HARDEST THING ABOUT BEING A WRESTLER?

THE MAT!

WHAT IS A CHEF'S FAVORITE WRESTLING MOVE?

THE SOUP-PLEX!

WHY DID THE WRESTLER JOIN THE CIRCUS?

HE WAS A RING MASTER!

WHY DID THE WRESTLER BRING A PENCIL TO THE MATCH?

TO DRAW A CROWD!

BOXING JOKES

WHY DIDN'T THE DOG WANT TO WRESTLE?

IT WAS A BOXER!

WHY IS IT CONFUSING TO WATCH TWO ELEPHANTS BOX?

THEY HAVE THE SAME COLOR TRUNKS!

WHY DON'T BAD BOXERS WEAR PANTS?

THEY DON'T HAVE ANY BELTS!

WHY DID THE BOXER REFUSE TO GO OUTSIDE IN WINTER?

HE DIDN'T WANT TO SLIP ON ICE AND GET KNOCKED OUT COLD!

WHY DID THE BOXER PUNCH HIS CLOCK OUT THE WINDOW?

TO SEE TIME FLY!

WHAT IS THE BEST SPORT TO LEARN WHEN YOU ARE MOVING?

BOXING!

WHY WAS THE BOXER FIRED FROM HIS JOB?

HE NEVER PUNCHED OUT!

MORE SPORTS JOKES

WHAT DOES A CYCLIST RIDE IN THE WINTER?

AN ICICLE!

WHY DID THE LACROSSE PLAYER GO TO JAIL?

BECAUSE HE SHOT THE BALL!

WHY DID THE WEIGHTLIFTER GET NEW CLOTHES?

SOMEBODY TOLD HIM HE WAS RIPPED!

WHY DO IMPATIENT PEOPLE HATE GOING TO THE GYM?

BECAUSE OF THE WEIGHTS!

WHAT DO HAIRDRESSERS DO IN THE WEIGHT ROOM?

CURLS!

WHAT DID THE JOCKEY SAY WHEN HE FELL OFF HIS HORSE?

I'VE FALLEN AND I CAN'T GIDDYUP!

WHAT DID THE ARCHER SAY WHEN SHE NEARLY GOT SHOT AT THE ARCHERY CONTEST?

WHOA, THAT WAS AN ARROW ESCAPE!

HOW DO BICYCLES HELP THE ENVIRONMENT?

BY RE-CYCLING!

WHAT GETS HARDER FOR ATHLETES TO CATCH WHEN THEY RUN?

THEIR BREATH!

WHY DID THE FIELD HOCKEY PLAYER BRING STRING TO THE GAME?

TO TIE THE SCORE!

WHY DID THE PICKLEBALL PADDLE BREAK UP WITH THE TENNIS RACKET?

IT COULDN'T HANDLE THE STRINGS ATTACHED!

WHICH SPORT IS ALWAYS GETTING INTO TROUBLE?

BADMINTON!

WHY DID THE OWNER NAME HIS RACEHORSE "BAD NEWS"?

BECAUSE BAD NEWS TRAVELS FAST!

WHAT SORT OF RACEHORSES COME OUT AFTER DARK?

NIGHT-MARES!

WHAT'S A HORSE'S FAVORITE SPORT?

STABLE TENNIS!

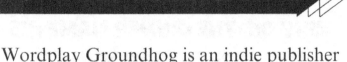

ABOUT WORDPLAY GROUNDHOG

Wordplay Groundhog is an indie publisher dedicated to making fun books for kids.

Wordplay Groundhog books are created by Chris Cate, a comedy writer and dad of three kids whose work has appeared in film, tv and many national media outlets. Parents may also know Chris' work from his popular *ParentNormal* memes and humor on social media where he has hundreds of thousands of followers.

Learn more about Wordplay Groundhog's joke books, picture books and upcoming chapter books at:

WORDPLAYGROUNDHOG.COM